Ssslay Girl, Slay

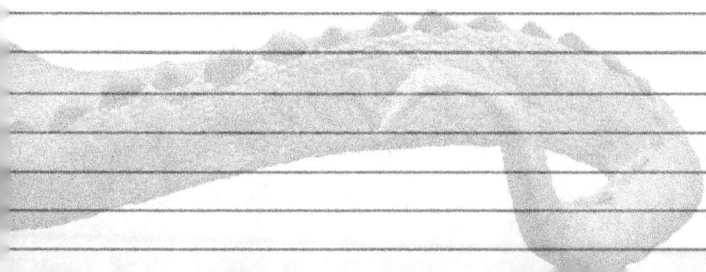

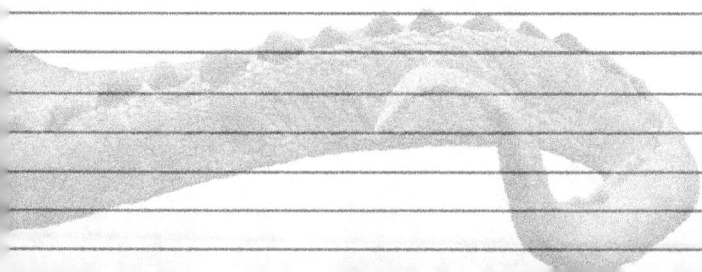

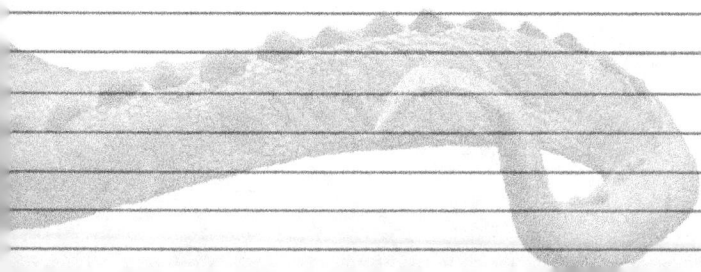

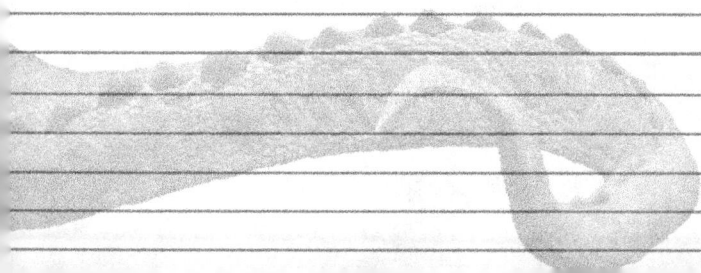

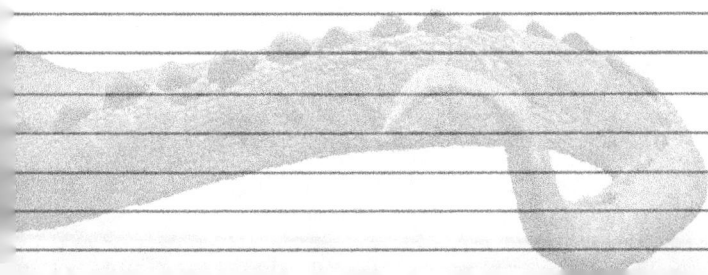

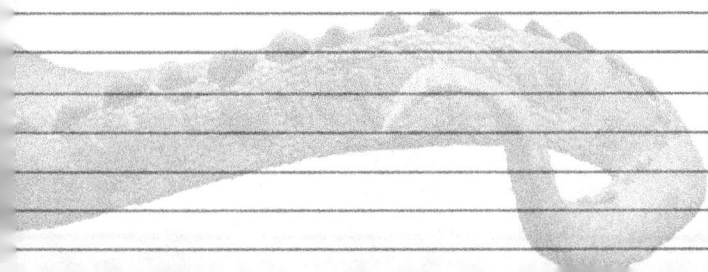

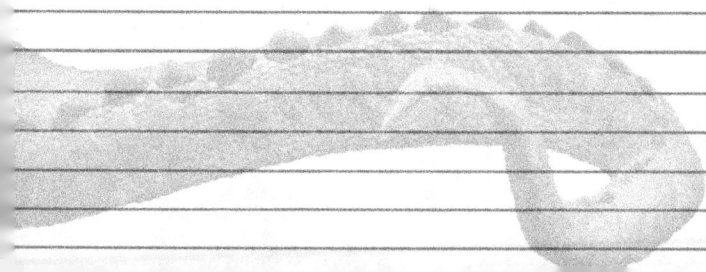

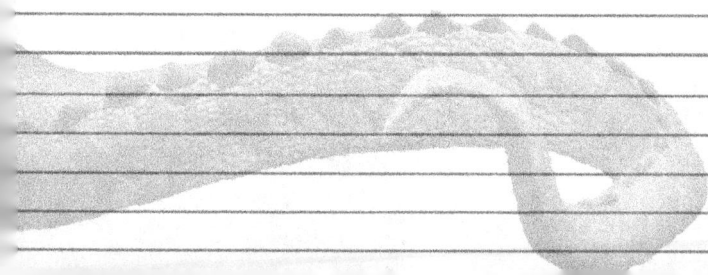

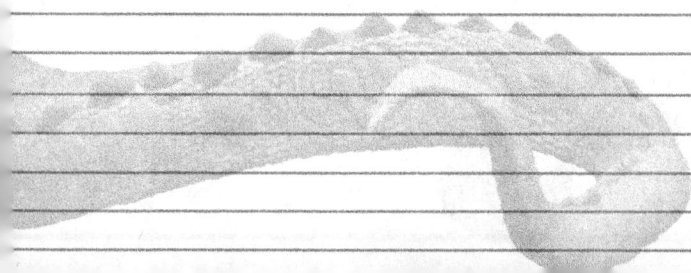

Ssslay Girl, Slay

by
Furry Godmother
...to the RESCUE

ISBN: 978-1-951221-06-5   Printed in the United States of America

FurryGodMotherSsslay@gmail.com
© 2019 Furry GodMother... to the RESCUE
All Rights Reserved

METAMORPHIC PRESS
metamorphicpress.com
illustration by Arju IT

www.ingramcontent.com/pod-product-compliance
Lightning Source LLC
Chambersburg PA
CBHW031601040426
42452CB00006B/372